LET'S JUST LAUGH AT THAT
FOR KIDS!

STEVE BACKLUND
with Brendon Russell, Janine Mason, Julie Heth, & Melissa Amato

© copyright 2015 Steve Backlund, Igniting Hope Ministries
www.ignitinghope.com
E-mail: kids@ignitinghope.com

Cover illustration: Scott Burroughs
Cover design: Robert Schwendenmann
Interior layout and formatting: Robert Schwendenmann, Julie Heth
Typesetting: Julie Heth
Author picture photography: Tracey Hedge
Contributing authors: Steve Backlund, Brendon Russell, Janine Mason, Julie Heth, Melissa Amato, Sally Schwendenmann
Editors: Melissa Amato, Julie Heth, Laurie Freeman
Special thanks to: Dusty May Taylor, Marcia Russell, Tom Harpham, Ryter family

ISBN-10: 0986309443
ISBN-13: 978-0-9863094-4-1

Please note that the author's publishing style capitalizes certain pronouns in Scripture that refer to Father, Son, and Holy Spirit and may differ from other publishers' styles.

LET'S JUST LAUGH AT THAT

FOR KIDS!

TABLE OF CONTENTS

INTRODUCTION

APPENDIX

LIES PAGE

ABOUT THE TEAM

STEVE BACKLUND

Steve is on staff at Bethel Church in Redding, CA. He and his wife Wendy founded Igniting Hope Ministries and travel extensively, equipping the body of Christ with hope, joy, and victorious mindsets. He is a contagious laugher, skilled in the art of destroying bad beliefs.

BRENDON RUSSELL

Brendon, a father of four, has spent many years serving in children's ministry. As a child, Brendon did not tolerate boredom well. It is his passion to make the Word of God as interesting and applicable as possible to help kids realize how fun and caring God is. As an intern for Steve (2014-2015), Brendon was a key player in seeing this book finalized.

JANINE MASON

Janine is someone who is passionate to see every child develop into everything that they are designed to be. With four children of her own, she has a passion for education and has spearheaded "Kingdom in the Classroom" initiatives at Bethel Church including workshops and conferences for educators.

JULIE HETH

Julie is the Project Manager for Igniting Hope Ministries and also has experience coordinating afterschool programs for kids in urban neighborhoods. Julie is passionate about seeing every child live with radical hope. She is someone who emanates love, joy, and hope to anyone who is fortunate to be around her.

MELISSA AMATO

Melissa has experience working with children as a pediatric ER nurse and a preschool teacher. She has taught performing and fine arts to children, led children's ministry, and much more. She lives to love and is passionate about seeing people of all ages walk in the abundant life Jesus paid for. Melissa is on staff at Bethel Church as Steve's assistant.

DEAR KIDS,

YOU CAN BE THE STAR OF YOUR LIFE!

Every good story has the star and the bad guy. In our life story, we get to be the star and overcome the bad guy – and the bad guys are not people who seem to be out to get us. The bad guys are lies we believe. When we believe lies, we settle for less than God's best. To be the best we can be, we need to destroy these lies and believe the truth about who God says we are. When we agree with God on something, we become unstoppable, but it will take some time and work. To become the star of our own life story, we must become fantastic lie detectives who sniff out lies that hold us back from the destiny God has for us.

The Bible makes it clear that we have an enemy (Satan) who is called the father of lies (John 8:44). He is scared of the power we have and tries his best to take us down, but he has no power except the ability to tell us lies. He tries to get us to believe false things about ourselves, others, and God.

Lies seem true inside our heads. One of the enemy's strategies against us is to make us think we are alone – that we are the only one who feels or thinks the way we do, and that things will never change. If we keep lies hidden, they're harder to get rid of. When we bring them into the open, we see them for what they are – stinky lies trying to stop us from getting to our destinies.

Psalm 2:4 says that God sits in the heavens and laughs. What is He laughing at? He is laughing at the enemy's plans and lies to destroy us. God knows the enemy doesn't have any real power, so He does not worry about his lies. Instead, He laughs at them.

In this book, we will learn to laugh with God at the lies that come against us to hold us back. We will use our laughter as a weapon against lies. The weapons in this book that are fueled by your laughter include: the Laughter Blaster, the Laugh-achine Gun, the Giggle Grenade, the Ha Ha Hammer, and the Laughter Boots.

When we laugh at lies, we start destroying the power they have. As the lies in our mind start to crumble, we then finish defeating the enemy by replacing the lie with the truths of God. In this book, we help you do that through verses from the Bible, declarations to speak, and practical activities to help you remember and know truth at a deep level.

Learning to destroy lies is pretty easy once we know how, but it doesn't happen all at once – it is a journey as we change what we believe a little at a time. It is like building a house. This looks really hard at first, but when we put down one brick at a time, we begin to see walls form. Before we know it, the house is complete! This is how it is with overcoming lies and believing truth. We can change the way we believe by dealing with one lie at a time. And we don't have to be perfect in the process. If we mess up and believe a lie again, we don't have to be discouraged. Failing doesn't make us a failure, it simply means we are learning to change the way we think.

WE KNOW YOU CAN DO IT!
YOU ARE A STAR!

DEAR PARENTS,

Picture what your life would have been like if, as a child, you hadn't believed any lies about yourself. Imagine if your insecurities weren't there about the way you looked or how smart or talented you were. Imagine if fear had no power because you disarmed it with the truth about how God sees you. Imagine if you had always believed God is good and He delights in you. Take a moment, and really let it play out in your mind. We would bet that you are sensing a greater freedom and joy than the reality of your childhood. Truth brings freedom and joy.

Many of us, as adults, still struggle to come to terms with the truth about ourselves, God, and the others around us. Our vision is to see a generation of young people walk in truth from an early age, knowing who they are and who their God is. It is possible, and it starts with us.

No matter how you define success, everyone wants it for the young people in their lives. We desire for them to have successful relationships with God and others, a successful education, and a successful career. Our hope for them is that they thrive and become the best version of themselves in every area of life. Our role in their lives now, and in preparing them for their future, cannot be underestimated. The Bible says train a child in the way they should go, and they will not depart from it (Proverbs 22:6). We have a responsibility to set them up for success by training them and giving them tools to have good beliefs.

Each one of us lives out of what we truly believe. We're not talking about what we think we believe at a head level, but we are talking about what we really believe at a deep down heart level. Children are no different. They react to the world around them and make decisions based on what they believe about

x

themselves, others, and God. We see their outward response and are sometimes mystified by their reactions, but we often fail to recognize that their actions come from an internal belief that is opposed to truth.

This book is a tool to help train the important children in our lives how to deal with the lies coming against them. These lies, if left unchecked, will rob them of their destiny and of thriving in life.

We believe it is possible to create an environment where it is normal to expose lies for what they are and to walk in truth. God's design is that children everywhere are trained in not just what to think and do, but also what to believe. Our dream is that our places of influence become places where it is normal to talk about what we believe, the lies we are facing, and the truth of God's Word.

We pray that as you read this book, radical breakthrough will come for you and your children. We dream of healthy families who will speak the truth to one another in love, and walk in tremendous joy because of it. We declare lies that have held kids captive will be exposed and neutralized as you laugh together. We declare that "Nothing is impossible!" will become your normal experience as a family. We release new levels of connection and freedom into your household that will affect not only your house, but also your whole neighborhood. We declare the kids you love will become a part of a new generation that takes God at His Word, believes the truth, and does amazing exploits in the earth.

BLESSINGS,
Steve, Brendon, Janine, Julie, and Melissa

HOW TO GET THE MOST OUT OF THIS BOOK

KNOW THAT YOU ARE BUILDING A CULTURE

This book is more than just another devotional to do with our kids. Instead, it is a tool to help us build a culture of truth and good beliefs. Changing the culture in our houses or classrooms is going to take a bigger commitment than just doing a devotional.

To make the most of this book, we encourage you to get involved with your kids. Do the activities and make declarations together. Look for opportunities to continue discussing what you have been learning without making it heavy. Keep fun at the center of what could otherwise be a heavy topic, and laugh together often.

IMMERSE YOURSELF IN THIS BOOK IN THESE WAYS

- Read it from start to finish with your children to get saturated with the truth.
- Reference particular chapters as you notice which lies your children are struggling with.
- Use this book as a weekly study. Pick one lie a week, memorize the scripture, make declarations during the week, and complete each action step.
- Read it with a group of children, and activate them in speaking truth and completing the action steps in creative ways.

TRUTHS TO UNDERSTAND THIS BOOK

GOD LAUGHS (PSALM 2:4)

What is God laughing at in this Psalm? He is chuckling at what His enemies are saying and planning. We can become more like God by laughing with Him at the ridiculousness of Satan's lies. The phrase "Let's Just Laugh at That" has the unusual ability to remove power from the enemy's lies and prepare our hearts for the truth. As a visual picture for the power of laughter, we have created laughter weapons with power to destroy lies. This enables us to see what is happening in the spirit realm as we laugh at lies instead of choosing to believe them.

THE BATTLE IS BETWEEN TRUTH AND LIES

John 8:32 tells us truth will make us free. The Kingdom of God is not moved forward primarily by good behavior, but by good beliefs. In working with children, we often focus on their behavior instead of their beliefs. However, if teach them to have good beliefs, good behavior will follow. We can teach a child how they should behave, but they will remain spiritually weak if they are believing lies. In each chapter, we share truths to believe in place of the lie. Knowing truth will build a foundation of good beliefs.

BRIGHT FUTURES COME FROM PRESENT GOOD BELIEFS

Romans 12:2 gives us an invitation into supernatural living. It says, "Let God transform you into a new person by changing the way you think." We transform our tomorrow by transforming our minds today. Intentionally renewing our minds with truth is a skill set that is vital for us and our children to learn to reach our full potential. We must not think, "Lord, tell me what to do," but rather, "Lord, tell me what to believe." Our children will be set up for success when we train them how to renew their minds, recognize lies, and believe truth.

KNOWING TRUTH BRINGS HOPE

Hope fills us at the moment we believe truth (Romans 15:13). Hope is what allows us to keep walking when we don't understand and positions us to step into faith. When we are believing truth, our hope level will be high. We can recognize if we are believing truth or lies by our hope level. We can increase our hope level by increasing our knowledge of God's truth. We will grow in hope as we grow in good beliefs.

WE HAVE TO LET GO OF SOMETHING IN ORDER TO LAUGH

To truly laugh at lies, we have to let go of some things, including bitterness, hurt, and unbelief. Children laugh more frequently than adults. This may be because they have lived fewer years and have less to let go of. When we teach children to laugh at lies when they are young, we can be confident they will use this skill far into their adult years. Learning to laugh at lies, instead of believing them, will prevent them from unnecessary hurt in the future. It is important to note that to be able to laugh at lies with our children, we have to remember that their current situation is not an indicator of our overall success as parents and teachers.

WALK IN LOVE AND WISDOM AS YOU LIVE A JOY-FILLED LIFE

We are to "Be happy with those who are happy and weep with those who weep" (Romans 12:15). We need to be sensitive to where children are at, and what is going on in their lives, as we seek to walk with them in increasing joy. Kids may really be having a hard time with the lies coming at them, and their circumstances may also be difficult. The tools in this book are to be used generously, but not apart from other tools like forgiveness, empathetic listening, clear communication, interactive discussions, and more.

WHAT IS IN EACH CHAPTER

THE TITLE

This is a "kingpin" lie. You may hear it come out of your child's mouth, or you may see the effects of it through how they are behaving. We urge you to read the lie out loud and laugh audibly. Something powerful happens when the lie is brought into the light through speaking it out loud.

THE STORY

Each chapter includes a short story that children may resonate with. Read it through with emotion, and consider discussing if they have ever felt the way described.

MORE LIES TO DEAL WITH

This is a list of other lies that are commonly connected to the kingpin lie. This helps kids identify more lies they could be believing. It will also help you, as a parent or leader, find the root of the lie. After reading the additional lies, we encourage you to ask kids what else they are believing in this area. This is a wonderful opportunity to guide them to ask the Holy Spirit to expose other lies.

THE TRUTH

We cannot simply get rid of a lie; we must replace it with the truth. In this section, biblical examples and promises are provided to refute the lies. We encourage you to read the Bible stories mentioned with your kids to get the truth lodged in their hearts.

WHAT CAN I SAY?

Romans 10:17 says faith comes by hearing. A key way to renew our minds is to declare the truth out loud. Remember that Jesus did not think His way out of the wilderness, but He spoke truth to counteract challenges concerning His identity and the nature of His Father (Matthew 4:1-11). Declarations will help our children do the same. We recommend you work with your children to make declarations a normal part of life. Find fun ways of doing them together, and help them make the connection when change is linked to the declarations they have been making. Look for opportunities daily to speak declarations over your children and with them.

WHAT CAN I DO?

This section provides three helpful steps to reinforce truth in the area the lie addresses. Your involvement with this section is the key to it being successful. We encourage you to not only provide the tools for them to do the activity, but also to take the time to invest in following up with them on how it went. Remember, you are helping them learn a new way of believing which will set them up for success.

HA! HA! HA! HA! HA! HA! HA! HA! HA! HA! HA! HA! HA! HA! HA! HA! HA! HA! HA! HA! HA! HA! HA! HA! HA! HA! HA! HA! HA! HA! HA! HA! HA! HA! HA! HA! HA! HA! HA! HA! HA! HA! HA! HA! HA! HA! HA! HA! HA! HA! HA! HA! HA! HA! HA! HA! HA! HA! HA! HA! HA! HA! HA! HA!

IT'S NOT FAIR

Have you ever thought you don't get as much as others? "My parents let my brothers and sisters do more than me. My friends get more than I do. The teacher gives other people special jobs, and I never get chosen!" As you think about these things, the warning light in your mind begins to flash. "What about me?!" You feel something rising inside you. Now it's fighting to get out of your mouth, and then these words cannot be held in any longer: "It's not fair!" As you say this, the siren sounds. Quick action is required. You pull out your weapon of choice – the Laughter Boots. You slip them on your feet and start stomping that lie to dust!

LET'S STOMP THESE LIES TO DUST!

IT'S NOT FAIR UNTIL EVERYTHING IS EQUAL.

EVERYONE GETS MORE THAN ME.

NOBODY CARES ABOUT MY NEEDS.

I NEED WHAT THEY HAVE TO MAKE ME HAPPY.

IF THEY ARE NOT FAIR TO ME,
I DON'T NEED TO BE FAIR TO THEM.

THE TRUTH

KEY VERSE

Philippians 4:6

"Don't worry about anything; instead, pray about everything. Tell God what you need, and thank Him for all He has done."

If we are only looking for things to be equal, life will never seem fair. There are several Bible stories that may not seem fair to us. One is when David goes to battle with 600 hundred men (1 Samuel 30). The battle is so long and hard that 200 hundred men had to rest by a stream. They left the others to fight. Later, the 400 men came back victorious. David asked for the treasure they won to be shared between the 600 men. Some of the fighters may have asked, "Why should these lazy men get anything?" They complained because they had done the work while the others rested. Still, David demanded it to be shared evenly.

Fair does not always mean equal. Even Jesus didn't spend the same amount of time with each of His disciples, but He knew what they needed. Jesus had twelve disciples, but He spent more time with three. If we look at what we don't have, life will never seem fair. Jesus might not give us what someone else has, but He always gives us what we need.

WHAT CAN I SAY?

- God always has the best for me.
- My life is special and unique. It will look different than anyone else's.
- I choose to think more about what I have than what I want.

WHAT CAN I DO?

- **Refuse to compare** - Comparing yourself to another person can steal your joy. Instead, don't worry about anything, but pray about everything (Philippians 4:6-7). Tell God what you need, and thank Him for all He has done. You will be amazed at how much better things will be.

- **Treat people well** - It starts with you. You get to change your world by treating people around you with honor (Luke 6:31). As you do this, you will often find people treating you more fairly. If you are waiting on someone else to treat you right first, then fairness may never happen. What is one thing you can do today to treat someone else well? Consider doing something like putting an encouraging note around your family's dinner plates or on their pillows before bed.

- **Celebrate the good stuff** - Do a happy dance over something you are grateful for. Sometimes we can have the most amazing things right in front of us and not realize what we have. If you're with family and friends, go ahead and have a party. Blow up balloons and put up decorations. There are plenty of things to celebrate. Invite your parents to enjoy the party with you.

GOD IS FAR AWAY

You are having one of those days. You know which kind of day – "a terrible, horrible, no good, very bad day." Everything feels bad, and all you need is someone to be your friend, to love you, and to tell you it is going to be okay. But today, to make things worse, no one is around, and you feel painfully alone. "At least Jesus loves me," you think to yourself, and a warm feeling starts to touch your heart. Then an icy blast rushes through. "But He's so far away," you hear. Your head drops, and your heart begins to ice over. Then you think, "No. I'm not falling for that lie." As you grab your Laugh-achine Gun, you shout aloud, "Your time is up, stinky lie! I'm going to demolish you!"

LET'S DEMOLISH THESE LIES TOO!

IF I CAN'T FEEL GOD'S PRESENCE, HE ISN'T HERE.

GOD LEAVES ME WHEN I DO SOMETHING WRONG.

GOD IS NOT A REAL FRIEND BECAUSE I CAN'T SEE HIM.

GOD IS TOO FAR AWAY FOR ME TO REALLY KNOW HIM.

HA! HA! HA! HA!
HA! HA!
HA!

THE TRUTH

"Teach
these new
disciples to
obey all the
commands
I have given
you. And be
sure of this: I
am with you
always, even
to the end of
the age."

The Bible says that God will never fail you or abandon you (Deuteronomy 31:6,8; Joshua 1:5). Do you know what *never* means? It means not ever. Not once. *It's not going to happen!* That's good news. It means that even when things are super tough, and it feels like God isn't there, He is still by your side. He is closer than the air you breathe.

Psalm 139 is a great part of the Bible for when it feels like God isn't near. It says that even if we were to try and hide from God, we couldn't! He is always near, and His thoughts towards us are always good. If you need more proof that there is nothing that can keep God away from you, Romans 8:38 tells us that nothing can separate us from His love.

God is called many different names. Each of them teach us something about who He is. One of the names of God is *Emmanuel*, and it means *God with us*. It's who He is and it doesn't change. He is *God with you*.

WHAT CAN I SAY?

- God is with me all the time.
- Nothing can separate me from God and His love.
- God loves to be with me.

WHAT CAN I DO?

- **Practice being aware of His presence -** We sometimes feel like God isn't with us because we don't believe He is. The more we believe He is with us, the more we will experience His presence and goodness. To remind yourself He is close, you can write a card that says, "God is with me" and put it in your pocket. You can also find something God created in nature to look at or hold. Choose something that reminds you of a promise God made to you. When you feel the card or the hold the object, you can remember He is with you.

- **Grow an attitude of thankfulness -** Being thankful helps us think like Jesus. Thinking like Jesus builds our faith and draws us closer to God. You can always find things to be thankful for. As you begin to praise and thank God, you will find that you become more aware of how close He is.

- **Build a friendship with God -** God is a good Father. He wants to be with you in every part of life – the good and the bad. Building a friendship with Him and talking to Him about everything makes it easier to know He is with you when things become difficult. Tell Him when you are happy and when you are sad, just like you do with other friends. Friendships take time to grow. Investing in your friendship with God will be the best thing you ever do.

BEING A CHRISTIAN IS BORING

Have you ever felt like being a Christian is just a list of rules? *Don't do that. Do this. Sit still in church. Pray and read your Bible more.* You think, "Is being a Christian all about trying to behave and following rules? I want to run, play, draw, have fun with my friends, get dirty, win at a game, and act just a bit crazy!" But then thoughts come to your mind: "God would not like any of that. He does not like me to have any fun. Being a Christian is boring." This is a sneaky lie! Let's get our Laughter Blaster and turn this lie into smithereens!

LET'S **BLAST** THESE LIES TOO!

ALL GOD WANTS IS FOR ME TO BEHAVE MYSELF.

YOU MISS OUT ON ALL THE FUN WHEN YOU'RE A CHRISTIAN.

GOD LIKES CHURCH TO BE BORING.

JESUS DOESN'T LIKE TO HAVE FUN LIKE I DO.

IT UPSETS GOD IF I HAVE FUN IN MY LIFE.

HA! HA! HA! HA! HA! HA!

THE TRUTH

KEY VERSE

Matthew 10:8

"Heal the sick, raise the dead, cure those with leprosy, and cast out demons. Give as freely as you have received!"

Jesus invented fun! Jesus came to give us a full life (John 10:10). He did a lot of miracles. He made the blind see and the lame walk. Now he says to us, "Why don't *you* try as well?" God also sent the Holy Spirit for us to team up with to change the world around us. Did you ever see a boring Christian in the New Testament? Paul (author of at least 13 books of the Bible) got shipwrecked and bitten by a poisonous snake, and he was not hurt. He spoke with powerful leaders, healed people from diseases, and changed many people's lives for the better.

Many New Testament characters had very exciting and action-packed lives (read Matthew, Mark, Luke, John, or Acts). It should not be any different for you! God wants to see you get the most out of every day. He is excited to have adventures with you.

WHAT CAN I SAY?

- God is not boring, and neither am I.
- Jesus told me to do the same things He did, and that's what I am going to do.
- There is nothing more exciting than hanging out with God!

WHAT CAN I DO?

- **Find out what God is really like** - Read the stories of Jesus and get to know God better. The New Testament is full of exciting stuff. Imagine being there as you read the stories. Also, you can ask people around you to tell you about their adventures with God. Miracles are still happening today, and you can be part of it.

- **Do what Jesus did** - God has amazing life-changing experiences waiting for you. Ask the Holy Spirit to help you as you and your family practice doing the miracles Jesus did. Offer to be part of His team so you can go on a lifelong adventure with Him.

- **Dream with God** - When you feel bored, dream about the amazing things you can do with God. It is fun to think of how you can help someone or even change a person's life for the better. You can share the good news of Jesus with others, pray for the sick, tell people stories of His goodness, and encourage people around you. Think about places you would like to go and things you want to do in your life. There are no limits to what you and God can do!

IT'S IMPOSSIBLE

HA! HA! HA! HA! HA! HA!

"I can't do it. It just won't happen. I have tried this more than a hundred times! Things will never change." Thoughts fill your head, and you can feel your hope running down the drain while disappointment gets dumped on you like a bucket of water. You feel like giving up and burying what you hoped was possible. Hang on! You need to ask yourself, "Who told me that?" That may be how you feel, but it doesn't mean it's true. Before you get carried away with your feelings, let's smash this trash with the Ha Ha Hammer.

LET'S SMASH AND TRASH THESE LIES TOO!

THE MIRACULOUS STORIES OF THE BIBLE DON'T HAPPEN TODAY.

NOT EVEN GOD KNOWS WHAT TO DO ABOUT THIS.

IF I HAVEN'T SEEN IT CHANGE, IT WON'T CHANGE.

GOD DOES MIRACULOUS THINGS FOR OTHERS, BUT NOT FOR ME.

IT'S TOO BIG! THERE IS NOTHING I CAN DO.

HA! HA! HA! HA! HA!

THE TRUTH

The Bible is filled from front to back with stories of the impossible becoming possible.

God created the world with words (Genesis 1), and He parted the Red Sea (Exodus 14). Jesus made blind people see and lame people walk (John 9, Mark 2). He raised people from the dead (John 11), and He fed 5,000 people with two loaves and five fish (Matthew 14).

There are hundreds of stories that seemed impossible until God showed up. He is the same God yesterday, today, and forever. He is just as powerful today as when Jesus walked on the earth.

God really, really likes you, and He likes it when His kids trust Him for impossible things (Luke 11:11).

WHAT CAN I SAY?

- There is always a way.
- The impossible is easy for God.
- My prayers are powerful.
- God gives me wisdom in impossible situations.

WHAT CAN I DO?

- **Build your faith** - Think of faith as a muscle. The more we use it, the more it will grow. Some ways we can build our faith include: declaring truth, hearing testimonies, and being thankful.

- **Don't let yesterday's mistakes stop you from being amazing today** - You may have had moments when you did not feel very successful. These can make you think other things are impossible for you also. This steals our hope for today. Here is an exercise to help with this: On pieces of paper, write down times in your life when you feel you have failed at something. Put them on the ground like stepping stones. Step on each one and notice that as you move forward, they are now behind you. The same is true of your past mistakes.

- **Give God something to work with** - Just like Peter had to get out of the boat to see if he could walk on water (Matthew 14:29), sometimes we need to take a risk. Faith is believing in what you cannot see or doing what cannot be done without God's help. Ask God what to do, believe for His strength, and then take a risk with Him. As you step out and take risks with God, the chances are high you will see a miracle!

I'M TOO YOUNG TO CHANGE ANYTHING

Have you ever felt powerless to change anything in the world because of how young you are? You watch TV and hear of all sorts of problems, and you can feel so small and so young. You think, "There are a lot of people in the world that need help!" As your brain starts to fill up with hopeless lies, a smile forms on your lips. You know what to do. You reach into your pocket and pull out your Giggle Grenade. As you pull the pin, you call out, "Say goodbye you filthy lies." *Boom!* The Giggle Grenade explodes into laughter and the lies are demolished.

LET'S TOSS A GIGGLE GRENADE AT THESE LIES!

I DON'T HAVE ANYTHING GOOD TO OFFER.

ONLY ADULTS CAN CHANGE IMPORTANT THINGS.

NO ONE WANTS TO LISTEN TO ME.

I AM NOT TAKEN SERIOUSLY.

CHILDREN HAVE A JUNIOR HOLY SPIRIT.

MY PRAYERS DON'T WORK.

HA!

HA!
HA!
HA!

THE TRUTH

KEY VERSE

1 Timothy 4:12

"Don't let anyone think less of you because you are young. Be an example to all believers in what you say, in the way you live, in your love, your faith, and your purity."

Have you heard of Miriam, the sister of Moses? Moses was put in a basket in the river (Exodus 2:3). Pharaoh's daughter (an Egyptian) found him, and Miriam stood close by to help arrange for Moses' mom to nurse him. Without the brave actions of Miriam, her baby brother may have never known his mother and who his real family was.

Then there is Josiah. He was only eight years old when he became king, and he changed a nation (2 Chronicles 34:1). He saw that Israel had drifted away from God, and he turned the whole nation back to Him.

When Jesus and His disciples fed 5,000 people with two loaves of bread and five fish (Matthew 14:13-21), guess who gave Jesus the fish and bread? A young boy!

Like Miriam, Josiah, and the boy with his fish and bread, you are never too young to make an impact.

WHAT CAN I SAY?

- God looks at my heart, not my age.
- I can make a real difference because of my love for God.
- I am not limited by my age or circumstances.
- The small things I do add up to great things.
- My age is great!

WHAT CAN I DO?

- **Get to know God well** - Talk to God and read His Word. Find out what pleases Him, and then do it. Jesus is looking for anyone who says yes to partnering with Him. He wants to do amazing things through you.

- **Pray for others** - As a child, you have great faith. Find people you can pray for, such as sick people, those who are sad, or people who need a miracle from God. You can move all of these mountains by praying with faith. Jesus said, "If you had faith as small as a mustard seed, you could say to this mountain, 'Move from here to there,' and it would move" (Matthew 17:20).

- **Do small things well** - If you can be trusted with the small things in life, you will be given more (Luke 16:10). Not only will God see you are trustworthy, but so will your parents and your teachers. Look for places you can help. When you do small things in a great way, you will be trusted with great things.

I NEED TO HANG OUT WITH THE POPULAR KIDS TO BE COOL

You're sitting in the lunchroom with your best friend, and you notice a group of kids walking by you, laughing. Every day they sit in the same place and never let other kids sit with them. They are the cool group. One day, they invite your friend to sit with them, and your friend leaves you. You begin to think you are not important and have thoughts like, "I need to sit with them to be cool, and I need to be cool!" *Beep, beep, beep!* Did you hear that?! It's the lie alarm. Let's grab the Laughter Boots and squish this lie.

LET'S SQUISH THESE LIES TOO!

BEING POPULAR IS THE MOST IMPORTANT THING IN LIFE.

ONLY COOL PEOPLE HAVE FUN.

COOL KIDS ARE BETTER THAN EVERYONE ELSE.

I HAVE TO LOOK LIKE OTHER PEOPLE TO BE LIKED.

I'LL NEVER BE POPULAR.

BEING POPULAR IS MORE IMPORTANT THAN BEING RESPECTED.

HA! HA! HA! HA! HA! HA!

THE TRUTH

Many times in the Bible, God told His people not to be afraid or worried because He was with them. He promised He would never leave them. This is a powerful truth to remember when we feel alone.

God is with you right now. He knows you. He knows what you're doing, what you like, and what you hope for tomorrow. He loves you! He loves everything about you. He also says we can talk to Him and know His voice (John 10:27), and He can help us with anything we are worried about (1 Peter 5:7).

God loves you today just as you are. And tomorrow, whether you are in the cool group or not, you will matter to Him. You are important, and He will be with you always. He was with John the Baptist (the one alone in the desert who paved the way for Jesus). He was with David (the kid watching the sheep alone, who killed the giant). He was with Matthew (the tax collector whom Jesus chose as one of His twelve disciples). He is with you too. You are important to Him and to those around you.

KEY VERSE

1 John 3:1

"See how very much our Father loves us, for He calls us His children, and that is what we are!"

WHAT CAN I SAY?

- I am a friend of God.
- God has a wonderful plan for my life.
- Earning respect is better than being liked.

WHAT CAN I DO?

- **Know that God loves you, and you are fully accepted** - God not only created everything, but He made us His children and became our Heavenly Father. As part of a family, you are always invited! God loves to be with you and does not hold back good things from you. You are His beloved child.

- **Dream with God** - Life is bigger than a group of popular kids. You may not be invited to all the places the popular kids are going to right now, but you are on a great adventure with your friend Jesus for life. Start writing down big dreams that you'd like to do with Jesus. Remember this: God has great things for you. He cares about your dreams, and He is more than able to help you accomplish them. Write down ten dreams. They can be anything from going to Disneyland to helping orphans! He cares about them all.

- **Make someone else feel included** - Other people may be feeling left out too, and you have the ability to help them feel included. Whether it is a brother, sister, cousin, neighbor, or friend at school, find someone that you can include into something you are doing this week. Some ideas for doing that are: 1) Invite someone to sit with you at lunch. 2) Be the first to be friendly. 3) Give a compliment.

IT'S MY PARENTS' JOB TO DO EVERYTHING FOR ME

You come home from school, dump your bag on the ground, and slump down at the dinner table. You are only concerned with eating your dinner and starting on homework. Your dad asks you about the day, and your mom reminds you of your dish duty. You grunt out loud, "But I have so much to do!" Your mom looks back at you with a look that says, "You're not getting out of this." The message is loud and clear. Though you're not brave enough to say it out loud, your brain cries out, "It's the parents' job to do everything for their children!" Knowing something is not quite right with your thinking, you reach for your trusty Laughter Blaster, aim, and "Ha ha!" The lie is ruined.

LET'S **BLAST** THESE LIES TOO!

I SHOULD BE ABLE TO RELAX AT HOME WHENEVER I WANT.

MY PARENTS SHOULD DO FOR ME WHAT OTHER KIDS' PARENTS DO FOR THEM.

IT'S TOO HARD.

I HAVE TO DO MORE THAN EVERYONE ELSE.

GOOD PARENTS GIVE THEIR KIDS EVERYTHING THEY WANT.

27

THE TRUTH

Now this may sound crazy, but doing things for others is good for us! Part of being respectful and honoring is being willing to help others around us. Did you know that when God said to honor your parents, it came with a promise? He said, "If you honor your father and mother, 'things will go well for you, and you will have a long life on the earth'" (Ephesians 6:3).

It has always been God's plan that we help each other, especially in families. If we don't do our part, then someone else has to or things don't get done.

Remember, your parents aren't the only ones who see what you are doing (Colossians 3:23), and there is a reward for those who freely give (Proverbs 11:25).

WHAT CAN I SAY?

- I respect my family.
- God loves my family and made us a team.
- I am generous toward my family, and I regularly help others.

WHAT CAN I DO?

- **Look for things to be thankful for** - Notice how much your parents do. Make a list of everything they provide, such as love, food, a home, education, and fun activities.

- **Believe your parents want the best for you** - Your parents want to help you become someone who is a blessing to the people around you. You start this by being a blessing to them by asking, "How can I help?" If you see dishes that need to be done or a table that needs to be cleared, ask, "Would you like me to do the dishes or clear the table?" Your parents want to stretch you and help you grow. Take on the challenge when given responsibility and be a "can do" person.

- **Speak with joy** - How do you sound when you speak? Ask yourself, "Are my words kind? Is how I say them kind?" Do everything with a joyful attitude. Practice telling people how you feel in a calm voice. You might be surprised by the better response you receive.

MY PARENTS ARE TOO STRICT

Friday has arrived! Your friends have planned for a group to go to the movies this evening, and you are invited. You see your parents after school and eagerly run up to give them the wonderful movie news. The look on their faces shows that they are not as excited as you are. Your face reddens as they try to explain why they don't think it is such a good idea. Thoughts about your parents enter your mind that make you angry. "They don't let me do anything," you start to mutter out loud. Then you realize, "I need to demolish these thoughts with the Ha Ha Hammer."

LET'S POUND THESE LIES WITH THE HA HA HAMMER!

I'M NOT ALLOWED TO DO ANYTHING!

MY PARENTS WON'T LET ME GROW UP.

I AM THE ONLY ONE WITH PARENTS LIKE THIS.

IF I ACT GRUMPY, THEY WILL GET THE
MESSAGE THAT THEY ARE UNFAIR.

HA! HA! HA! HA! HA!

THE TRUTH

KEY VERSE

Matthew 19:14

"But Jesus said, 'Let the children come to me. Don't stop them! For the Kingdom of Heaven belongs to those who are like these children.'"

How do you feel when you see another child being disrespectful, rude, or demanding? Do you find it uncomfortable to watch? Your parents have been given the awesome job of raising and shaping you to be the best you can be. Every parent might have a different idea on how this is done, but believe it or not, they want the best for you.

The boundaries parents set will actually give you freedom. When your parents keep you safe, you have the freedom to dream, create, and play without having to be fearful.

Let's be funny for a moment. Say you are in the jungle with wild animals all around. Do you think you will paint a picture, go swimming, or play tag? Probably not. But if your parents built a house in the jungle with an animal-proof fence around it, are you more likely to paint, swim, or play? Yes! In the same way, the decisions your parents make are like an "animal-proof fence" around you so you can live life in joy and freedom. The safety they provide gives you an opportunity to be your best!

WHAT CAN I SAY?

- My parents want the best for me.
- Honoring my parents is a great thing to do.
- I am thankful my parents want me to be safe.
- Boundaries bring safety and real freedom.

WHAT CAN I DO?

- **Understand how to get greater freedom** - Greater freedom comes from being responsible. The best way to have more freedom tomorrow is to be trustworthy today. If your parents can trust you today to do the right things, then it is more likely they will give you more freedom in the future.

- **Think about what you get to do** Make a list of the activities and hobbies you get to do. Tell your parent(s) about the best trip or activity you can remember doing together. Create a plan for what you want to do as you get older. Let them know your dreams and ideas.

- **Enjoy being a kid** - You probably don't have to worry about nearly as much as your parents. You don't have to think about getting food, money, or clothes. Enjoy the free time you have to play, create, and dream. You have a special faith and special value to God. Enjoy being young.

LYING WILL SOLVE MY PROBLEMS

Here it comes. You have nowhere to hide! How are you going to escape? What are you going to say to get out of this one? You did something wrong, you know people are going to find out, and you want to hide it from everyone! You think, "Oh man, if anyone finds out, I am in trouble! I have to lie! There's no way out. Lying will solve my problems!" In this moment, you know what to do. You reach for your laughter bullets and load them into your Laugh-achine Gun. You square up and pull the trigger. "Ha ha!" This lie is demolished.

LET'S SHOOT THESE LIES DOWN!

LYING WILL MAKE ME FEEL BETTER.

LYING IS NOT A BIG DEAL.

LYING DOESN'T HURT MY RELATIONSHIPS.

A HALF-TRUTH IS NOT A LIE.

IF NO ONE KNOWS, LYING IS OKAY.

HA! HA! HA! HA! HA! HA! HA!

THE TRUTH

KEY VERSE

John 14:6

"Jesus told him, 'I am the way, the truth, and the life. No one can come to the Father except through Me.'"

God tells us not to lie because He wants to protect us. He wants to have a close relationship with us, and He knows what's best for us. Lying hurts our relationships with our family, teachers, and friends. It destroys trust. However, telling the truth builds trust. Being truthful is more important than having great treasure.

God gives us the ability to know right from wrong. He made us strong in spirit so we can do what is right, even when it is scary. God's love and power will help us be courageous to tell the truth (2 Timothy 1:7).

Sometimes we lie because we feel pressured, and other times we lie on purpose. All of us have probably lied in some way, but those who develop a pattern of lying will have great difficulty in life. If we have lied, there is hope for us. God can turn it into good if we don't try to hide it but tell the truth, learn from our mistakes, and make things right with God's help.

WHAT CAN I SAY?

- I am a truth-teller!
- Even if I don't know the "right thing" to say, I can tell the truth.
- Telling the truth makes my relationships strong.

WHAT CAN I DO?

- **Value truth** – You may think lying is helping you in the moment, but it has bad effects. Picture a treasure chest that holds trust. Every time you tell the truth, you are putting treasure into that chest. The more treasure you have, the more trust you build. The more trust you build, the more freedom you have.

- **Know truth** – Get to know Jesus. To become a super truth-teller, you need strength and courage. Jesus is the way, the truth, and the life (John 14:6). In moments when you feel you need to lie, do this: stop, think, ask Jesus for His help, and then do the right thing. He will give you strength to tell the truth even when it's hard.

- **Tally the truth** – Every time you are tempted to lie and you choose to tell the truth, put a tally on a piece of paper. When you reach five tallies, celebrate your master truth-telling skills. Tell a parent or your teacher about one of those times, and why you chose to tell the truth.

MY WORDS AREN'T POWERFUL

HA! HA! HA! HA! HA!

Imagine you are walking around the neighborhood one day, and you see a group of kids standing together. One looks really upset, and you realize it is because everyone else is making fun of him. You think to yourself, "I should say something." Then you think further, "But that kid is kind of weird. If I did stick up for him, it wouldn't matter anyway. My words aren't powerful." Then *bam!* You realize you've been hit with a lie! "I could help that kid!" You feel courage rise in you to help, so you throw on your Laughter Boots and stomp the power out of that lie with a mighty "Ha ha."

LET'S STOMP THESE LIES TOO!

IT'S NOT BAD IF EVERYONE ELSE IS SAYING IT TOO.

IF I SAY I AM KIDDING, IT MAKES IT OKAY.

I'M NOT RESPONSIBLE FOR WHAT I SAY.

MY WORDS DON'T CHANGE ANYTHING POSITIVELY OR NEGATIVELY.

THE TRUTH

God spoke the entire universe into being by His words! He said, "Let there be light," and there was light (Genesis 1:3). He commanded the land to have trees and plants, and they grew (Genesis 1:11).

James tells us that our tongue is like a rudder that steers a ship (James 3:4). Our words direct our lives. If we consistently use negative words, our ship most likely will be shipwrecked. When we speak positively, we will begin to think more positively and behave more positively. Our beliefs and words combined are a powerful weapon to change things around us.

Our tongues have the power of life and death (Proverbs 18:21). We can bring freedom to our lives and others around us, or we can put roadblocks up with our words (James 3:1-12).

KEY VERSE

Proverbs 18:21

"The tongue can bring life or death."

WHAT CAN I SAY?

- My words are powerful.
- I bring positive change through my words.
- I choose to speak words of life.

WHAT CAN I DO?

- **Do an experiment** - Buy two of the exact same seedling plants. Take care of them the same way, using water and sunlight. Speak mean words to one and kind words to the other every day. Keep doing this daily and check them in 3-4 months.

- **Speak life** - See what you can change with your words. Pick an area of your life you want to grow in. Make declarations to change the way you think about it. Say them every day until you see change

- **Kill negativity with kindness** - Pick out someone you haven't been getting along with lately or someone who seems sad. Decide to speak kind things to that person this week. Try it at least three times, and then look for improvement in the way they are responding to you. Even if you don't see an outward change, believe you do change lives with your words.

I'M STUPID

HA! HA! HA! HA! HA! HA! HA!

It keeps happening. Your brother asked you a question, and you didn't know what to say. Your teacher put a red mark on your paper and told you to redo a question. Your report card came back, and it was all poor grades. Then a kid at recess says out loud, "You're stupid!" You think of all your mistakes, and you start to believe it. The thought feels more and more real as it runs through your head. Then you say it too. "I don't do anything right. I am stupid." But wait! You know it's not true. It's time to pull out the Ha Ha Hammer and flatten that lie like a pancake.

LET'S FLATTEN THESE LIES TOO!

I ALWAYS MESS UP.

BECAUSE I STRUGGLE IN SCHOOL, IT MEANS I'M STUPID.

EVERYONE ELSE IS SMARTER THAN ME.

IF I DON'T KNOW SOMETHING, IT MEANS I HAVE A BAD BRAIN.

IF I FEEL STUPID, IT MEANS I AM STUPID.

THERE IS NOTHING I CAN DO TO INCREASE MY INTELLIGENCE.

HA! HA! HA! HA! HA!

THE TRUTH

KEY VERSE

1 Corinthians 2:16

"For, 'Who can know the Lord's thoughts? Who knows enough to teach Him?'"

God is smart. Of course He is, right? Did you know that you were made in the image of God? God created Adam and Eve, and all people in His own image (Genesis 1:27). God made us to be like Him, and as Christians, we even have the mind of Christ (1 Corinthians 2:16). This means we can also think like Him. Therefore, we should not say we are stupid. This is a serious word that is hurtful to ourselves and others (Matthew 5:22).

How do we know when we are smart? It's not just when we get good grades. It's when we act wisely in daily life. We are truly smart when we think like Jesus and make good decisions in life.

God gave you a good brain. Don't forget that your brain is like a muscle. It can grow stronger and smarter. Muscles don't grow by looking at other people's muscles. Muscles grow from exercise. Comparing your smarts to others will only make you feel bad. Grow your smarts by working out your brain, and encourage others to do the same.

WHAT CAN I SAY?

- My brain thinks right and understands what it needs to understand.
- Every day I get wiser.
- I love learning, and it's not scary to try new things.

WHAT CAN I DO?

- **Celebrate your strengths** - We are often quick to beat ourselves up if we get something wrong, but how often do we celebrate getting something right? At the end of each day, think of three things you did really well. Clap for yourself, and tell your parents about one of them.

- **Pray over your body** - Put your hands on your head and say this: "I bless my brain! I have a passion to learn. I am wise in my actions. I make good decisions. I think well." Do this every day when you wake up in the morning.

- **Exercise your brain** - There are things you can do to get smarter. Reading is the best way. Readers are leaders! Other ways to do this are to do puzzles, build things, practice math, listen to a talk on a new subject, and solve riddles.

I'M NOT GOOD AT ANYTHING

"I feel like such a loser," you think. You've tried playing sports or doing music, and it seems like everyone is better than you. You start to wish you could be more like them – faster, smarter, and more talented. It seems each one of them is amazing at something. In your mind you see them being lined up and awarded a medal for being the best at what they are good at. "Argh," you shout on the inside. "It stinks to be me. I'm not good at anything!" Wait just a minute. It's time to grab that rotten lie and throw it in the trash can. Toss a Giggle Grenade in after it and slam the lid down. "Ha ha." No lie can withstand that!

LET'S TRASH AND BLAST THESE LIES TOO!

GOD CAN'T USE ME IF I AM NOT AS TALENTED AS OTHERS.

I DON'T HAVE ANY TALENTS.

GOD ONLY WORKS WITH THOSE WHO LOOK TALENTED.

IF I DON'T FEEL TALENTED I AM NOT TALENTED.

PEOPLE WHO ARE TALENTED DON'T HAVE TO WORK AT IT.

HA!

HA!

HA!

HA!

THE TRUTH

KEY VERSE

Philippians
4:13

"I can do
everything
through
Christ, who
gives me
strength."

You were made by God! The Bible says that while you were still inside your mother, God was watching you grow and getting excited about the life you would have (check out Ephesians 2:10, Jeremiah 1:5, and Psalm 139). When He was planning out what you would look like and what personality you would have, He was also planning the talents He would place inside you. You were put together by the Creator of the whole universe, and He doesn't make any mistakes.

It's easy to look around us and believe that our friends or siblings have more important talents than us. When we think this, we can fall into the trap of believing that we don't have anything good to offer the world around us. The truth is we are all different, and we have many differences we still need to discover that are valuable to the world (1 Corinthians 12:14-31).

WHAT CAN I SAY?

- I have everything I need to change the world around me.
- Because I have a unique mission, I have unique talents.
- I work hard to grow my talents.

WHAT CAN I DO?

- **Discover your talents** - Make a list of the talents God gave you. Ask your parents, teachers, coaches, or other leaders to help you. Ask them to share with you what talents they believe God has given you. Then choose to trust that God has gifted you in these areas.

- **Increase your talent** - Even gifted people have to work at their gift. No one becomes excellent at their talents without working at them. Ask God how you can best use your talents and spend time practicing to make them even stronger.

- **Celebrate your talents and others** - Recognize the good in the people around you and celebrate the way they show God in their lives. Do the same for yourself. Make a poster or screen saver for your phone or computer that celebrates who you are.

GOD ONLY CARES ABOUT THE BIG THINGS IN LIFE

Have you ever thought, "God, what do you think of me doing this? Should I be doing something more important for you?" You can start to feel bad when you are enjoying what you like. Lies jump into your head telling you to stop having fun and start doing the big things in life. Uh oh. You need to act quickly. You pull out the Laugh-achine Gun, find your laughter bullets, and destroy these lies.

LET'S DESTROY THESE LIES TOO!

GOD GETS ANGRY WHEN I JOKE AND PLAY.

I AM NOT IMPORTANT ENOUGH FOR GOD TO CARE.

WHAT'S IMPORTANT TO ME IS NOT IMPORTANT TO GOD.

GOD IS TOO BUSY TO THINK ABOUT ME.

HA! HA! HA! HA! HA! HA! HA!

LJLAT

THE TRUTH

David is a Bible character who knew how to enjoy himself. He liked slingshots, played music on his harp, danced, and wrote songs. God enjoyed seeing David doing what gave him joy, and it just so happened that some of the fun things David did helped make history. The slingshots he was once fascinated by actually became a weapon that he killed a giant with and saved his whole nation (1 Samuel 17).

The truth is that God cares about your hobbies and interests. He actually made you to have unique interests and desires, and none of these are to be considered unimportant.

Have you ever looked at nature really closely (I mean really looked)? God is a big God, but He also loves the small things. He created living things so small that we cannot even see them. He even created very tiny things in our body to give us life.

So yes, there are big things in life we can do that need doing, but we can know God puts great value on the little things as well.

WHAT CAN I SAY?

- God cares about big things and small things.
- God cares about what I like.
- God delights in me.

WHAT CAN I DO?

- **Find out what activities make you happy** - Take a moment to think about the activities you enjoy. Ask yourself two questions: Is this hurting me? Am I hurting others when I do this? If you can answer no to both, then celebrate this part of your life.

- **Experience God's delight** - Ask God how He feels about the things you enjoy. God is excited to tell you about how much He loves you and what you enjoy. Picture how a parent gets excited about something big or small their child has done. See that smile on Jesus' face as you ask Him how He feels.

- **Practice what you enjoy** - Now that you know what healthy activities bring you joy, develop a plan to grow these talents in your life. Like David and his slingshot, your talent might lead you to do something to change the world.

I CAN'T CONTROL MY ANGER

Does the "Hulk" live at your house, or inside of you? The Hulk is a character who changes when he gets mad. He turns green, gets bigger, and smashes things that get in his way. Sometimes when you get mad you may look a bit like the Hulk. Maybe you don't turn green, but you look scary to others around you and do things you normally wouldn't do. Some situations make you so angry. At first, the anger bubbles inside you, but pretty soon it is red hot and you are ready to explode. "They better be nice to me," you think. "I am mad, and when I'm like this, I can't control my anger." Oh no. This slimy lie is trying to take you down. Grab your Laughter Blaster. Let's vaporize that thing!

LET'S **VAPORIZE** THESE LIES TOO!

EVERYBODY GETS MAD, SO IT IS OKAY.

IT'S NORMAL TO ACT BADLY WHEN I'M MAD.

SHOUTING OR SLAMMING THE DOOR WHEN I AM ANGRY MAKES THINGS BETTER.

I HAVE A RIGHT TO BE MAD AND TO LET PEOPLE KNOW IT!

I CAN BEST CHANGE THINGS BY GETTING MAD.

HA! HA! HA! HA! HA! HA!

THE TRUTH

The Bible tells us to not sin when we are angry (Ephesians 4:26). Even the Bible knows that we will get angry, but there is a way to feel anger and still not sin. We all have things that happen that make us feel angry or upset. Have you noticed how it feels to be around someone else who is mad or very, very unhappy? It feels uncomfortable. Learning how to handle ourselves when we feel angry means we are becoming more like Jesus.

Anger becomes a sin when we lose self-control, causing us to make poor choices and hurt the people around us. Self-control is a fruit of the Spirit. It comes from being close to Jesus (Galatians 5:22-23). Unlike the Hulk, who only has anger inside and it controls him, you have the Holy Spirit inside you, who gives you the gift of self-control!

KEY VERSE

Proverbs 15:1

"A gentle answer deflects anger, but harsh words make tempers flare."

56

WHAT CAN I SAY?

- I am patient and self-controlled.
- I am responsible for me. I don't blame others when I get angry.
- The Holy Spirit helps me stay calm even when I feel angry.

WHAT CAN I DO?

- **Know yourself** - Learn to recognize and deal with your anger before it gets red hot and hard to manage. Don't wait until you are bubbling over and out of control to take positive action. Make a list of the events that usually make you mad. Share your list with someone who manages their anger well.

- **Make a plan** - Find out what helps you to calm down and make a plan for times when anger starts to rise up inside of you. Some examples of what you can do are: walk away, get alone, find someone to talk to, read your Bible, listen to music, pray, or make declarations.

- **Detect lies** - Sometimes when we get super mad, it is because the enemy is shouting at us. He takes one negative circumstance and makes us think everything is wrong! Become a lie detective to discover what lies you have been told that are making you feel this angry, then replace them with the truth.

I'M THE ONLY ONE WHO FEELS LIKE THIS

A feeling drops in your stomach. It is a feeling mixed with fear and loneliness. You would hate for your friends to find out. Surely they would make fun of you if they knew. You look at the people around you, and they are so confident. They look like they have it all together and always know what to do. You begin to think about finding a place to hide. You are convinced there is something wrong with you. Others don't seem to have any problems. "I'm the only one who feels like this." What? Where did that thought come from? This is a big fat lie that has just tried to slime you. It's time to pull out the Giggle Grenade and blast that goo into space.

LET'S BLAST THESE LIES INTO SPACE!

ALL THE OTHER KIDS HAVE GOT IT TOGETHER.

THERE IS SOMETHING WRONG WITH ME.

I'M THE ONLY ONE WHO WORRIES ABOUT FITTING IN.

THINGS WILL NEVER CHANGE.

NO ONE UNDERSTANDS HOW I FEEL.

THE TRUTH

God and people care about what you are feeling and thinking. We are children of God, but sometimes we still face hard things. There are a lot of feelings we can have such as happiness, excitement, sadness, fear, worry, and many more.

When we hide things we feel, people cannot get to know us, and they cannot help us when we need it. One way we can love like Jesus loved is to share our thoughts and emotions with our family and special friends.

Everyone feels scared of something. You might feel fear when you walk into a new classroom or when you try out for a sport. You are not alone in feeling like this. It only seems like you are because people often hide their fears.

You are brave. Stand strong and don't let your fear cause you to miss out. The Holy Spirit lives in you and wants to comfort you and make you brave.

KEY VERSE

Proverbs 29:25

"Fearing people is a dangerous trap, but trusting the Lord means safety."

60

WHAT CAN I SAY?

- What God thinks about me is the most important thing.
- I am not alone in my feelings.
- Even when I'm scared, I move forward.

WHAT CAN I DO?

- **Talk to God** - Tell Him how you feel, what you're afraid of, and what you are worried about. Be honest with Him. He won't get angry. He is a kind, loving God who wants the best for you.

- **Ask people questions** - Find out from your parents or people you trust if they have ever felt the way you feel. You might be surprised by the answer. You are not alone in your feelings. Ask them how they felt and what they did to deal with the feelings they had.

- **Think more about the feelings of others** - There are boys and girls around you who are wondering if they will ever be comfortable around people. Love them and encourage them. As you help others with their feelings, your own feelings about yourself will get better.

I'M NOT IMPORTANT

"I have an idea. I have an idea! Hello? Is anyone listening to me?" You are working on a group project in school, and your classmates aren't listening to you. You have tried to speak up two or three times, but they keep acting as if you hadn't said anything at all. You start thinking that the group doesn't need you there. You wonder if you got up and left, would your teacher even notice? Then more thoughts begin to ring in your head... "No one cares. I'm not important." This a great time to take out your Ha Ha Hammer and pound this lie until it turns into powder, and then blow it away!

LET'S POUND THESE LIES INTO POWDER!

WHAT I SAY AND WHAT I DO DOESN'T MATTER.

I'M NOT SPECIAL.

NO ONE NEEDS ME OR EVEN THINKS ABOUT ME.

IF I WASN'T HERE, NO ONE WOULD NOTICE.

HA! HA! HA! HA! HA!

THE TRUTH

KEY VERSE

John 15:16

"You didn't choose me. I chose you. I appointed you to go and produce lasting fruit, so that the Father will give you whatever you ask for, using My name."

Imagine a beach and all its grains of sand. God has more kind and loving thoughts about you than the number of grains of sand on the beach (Psalm 139:17,18). That's a lot of good thoughts! God thinks you are special. He knows everything about you, including how many hairs are on your head (Luke 12:7)!

God loves you. You are so important that He sent His only Son, Jesus, for you (John 3:16), and Jesus gladly gave His life for you (John 10:11). You matter so much that you are worth dying for. Jesus rose from the dead! He is that powerful, and He loves you.

You bring something special to the world, and the world needs you. You are an important part of God's family. You are a world changer!

WHAT CAN I SAY?

- I am important!
- I am one of a kind.
- I am needed in God's family.

WHAT CAN I DO

- **Learn about world changers** - Read (or ask your parents to read you) stories of people who have changed the world. As you read, remember that you are no different. You can make a difference in the lives of others now. Even small things that you do well now can make a really big difference.

- **Expose the lie** - Let your parents or a good friend know that you are hearing this lie, and ask them to tell you why you are important. Write down what they say so that you can read it later and remember it.

- **Celebrate you** - Make a poster or some other artwork that shows what is special about you and hang It on your wall. Whenever you look at it, you can remember how special you are and thank God for how He made you.

I'M UGLY

HA! HA! HA! HA! HA! HA! HA!

"They are *so* beautiful," you think in disgust. You feel sick about the fact that everyone you see on TV is perfect, and you're not. You think to yourself, "I'm ugly. I will never succeed in life looking like this." You have big dreams for who you want to be and what you want to do when you grow up, but it seems impossible. You hate the way you look, and you feel your looks will hold you back forever. It's time to pull out your Laughter Blaster and blast these ridiculous lies away!

LET'S BLAST THESE LIES TO BITS!

PEOPLE DON'T LIKE ME BECAUSE OF MY LOOKS.

GOD DOESN'T LIKE THE WAY I LOOK.

I WILL NEVER DO ANYTHING IMPORTANT BECAUSE I AM UGLY.

GOD MADE A MISTAKE WHEN HE MADE ME.

I'M NOT AS GOOD AS OTHERS BECAUSE OF THE WAY I LOOK.

HA! HA! HA! HA! HA! HA!

67

THE TRUTH

"Thank you
for making
me so
wonderfully
complex! Your
workmanship
is marvelous
– how well I
know it."

Zacchaeus was a very short man. He was so short that when he was in a crowd, he couldn't see Jesus because everyone was taller than him. Zacchaeus decided to climb a tree so he could see Him. Jesus saw Zaccheus in the tree and called for him to come down. Jesus wanted to visit his house and spend time with him. Even though he probably didn't like how short he was, Zacchaeus did not let this stop him from his destiny.

You too might have things you don't like about the way you look. You may not like the size of your nose, the way your hair looks, the shape of your body, or the color of your eyes. We need to understand that most people wish they looked different in some area, so we are not alone in how we feel. But there is good news we can remember: we are made in the image of God.

You are God's child and children look like their parents. All that God makes is good, and that includes you! God made you and knows everything about you. He created a piece of art when He made you, and He knows and loves every detail of how you look (see Psalm 139:1-5 and 13-15).

WHAT CAN I SAY?

- God loves the way I look, and what He thinks matters most.
- My looks don't hold me back.
- I like the way I look.

WHAT CAN I DO?

- **Become beautiful on the inside** - It is impossible to become good-looking on the inside without it showing up on your face! As you grow older, you will most likely hear messages that being good-looking is the most important thing in life. This is a lie. Decide now that you will focus on becoming beautiful on the inside and letting God show it on the outside.

- **Brush and flush** - Every time you hear, "I'm ugly" or "You're ugly," just brush and flush. Brush that lie off your shoulder, throw it in an imaginary toilet, and flush it down the drain. Then ask someone you trust what is good-looking about you. Ask Jesus how He sees you. Record this in a journal or write it on your mirror, and read it out loud every time you see yourself.

- **Learn how to improve your appearance** - Even though we don't want to think too much about our looks, it is still important to live a life of excellence – including our appearance. Learn to take care of yourself by consistently brushing your teeth and hair, eating healthy foods, and exercising.

I DON'T HEAR FROM GOD

Silence. Nothing. "Are you there?" You were in Sunday school this morning, and one of the other kids was talking about hearing from God. You have tried before, and it didn't seem to work. The only thing you thought you heard was your own voice. Suddenly lies come into your head: "God doesn't want to talk to me. Even if He did, I wouldn't be able to hear Him." You wonder why He makes it so hard to hear His voice. Then you remember that God is good! These are lies in your head, and it's time for a Giggle Grenade! You pull the pin, toss the grenade into the middle of the lies, and watch them explode!

LET'S EXPLODE THESE LIES INTO DUST!

I DON'T KNOW HOW TO HEAR GOD'S VOICE.

IT'S HARD TO HEAR GOD.

I CAN ONLY HEAR HIM WHEN I'M IN CHURCH.

I AM SPIRITUALLY DEAF.

GOD HAS GIFTED OTHERS TO HEAR HIM BETTER THAN ME.

IT'S NOT REALLY GOD SPEAKING TO ME.

HA!

HA!
HA!

HA!

THE TRUTH

Some people think God only talks to grown ups, but Samuel was a child when the Lord began talking with him. In fact, when Samuel first heard God's voice, he thought it was his friend Eli speaking to him, not God. Eli is the one who told Samuel that it was the Lord talking to him. Once Samuel knew that it was God, he began to learn how to recognize His voice (see 1 Samuel chapter 3 for the whole story).

Our Heavenly Father wants to talk to His kids. Like Samuel, you can learn to hear His voice and grow in believing it is really Him speaking to you. It's that easy!

God made us with spiritual eyes to see and spiritual ears to hear. He speaks to us in a voice we can understand and recognize (John 10:3-4). Our Heavenly Father loves to speak to His children and give us words to direct our lives, and to encourage ourselves and others. When we speak encouragement to others, it is sometimes called prophecy. We can all prophesy words of life to others (1 Corinthians 14:1-3, 39). The Lord has called us to hear Him for others and for ourselves. We can have confidence we hear His voice in great ways.

"Let love be your highest goal. But you should also desire the special abilities the Spirit gives – especially the ability to prophesy."

WHAT CAN I SAY?

- It's easy for me to hear God's voice.
- I hear God clearly, and He likes to talk to me.
- I can encourage others and hear God's heart for them.

WHAT CAN I DO?

- **Love the Bible** - There are many ways we can grow in hearing God's voice, but the most important way is to read the Bible. God will never speak to us anything that is against the Bible. Also, we get to know His heart for us by reading the Bible because the Holy Spirit will make the Bible come alive for us.

- **Practice listening to God's voice** - Ask Him what He's saying, and then tell someone you trust what you're hearing. Thank God out loud that He is helping you hear His voice. To learn new ways He might be speaking to you, talk to strong Christians you know and find out the different ways they hear God.

- **Encourage someone today** - Ask God how He wants to encourage someone. You can ask Him for a phrase, a scripture, or a picture that would bring them hope and strength. Then tell them what you believe He is saying. Ask them what it means to them. Tell them words that build them up, cheer them up, and/or draw them near to God (1 Corinthians 14:3).

GOD IS MAD AT ME

You are standing with your face in the corner. You earned a timeout yet again. Thinking over the day, you remember the poor choices you have made. "I told a lie. I hit my sister. My room is still a mess. Oh man! I think everyone is mad at me – my teacher, my sister, and my parents." Then you start to get upset and wonder, "Is God mad at me? Oh yes, He is. He must be. I am getting punished because God is mad." A fight rises in you, and you think, "That can't be true!" You remember that you have your Laugh-achine Gun, and now would be a great time to use it. You pull it out and blast that lie with laughter!

LET'S SHOOT THESE LIES DOWN!

GOD IS IMPATIENT.

GOD WILL BE MAD AT ME IF I MAKE MISTAKES.

GOD IS MAD AT ME AND MADE MY DAY TURN OUT BAD.

IF I'M SICK OR HURT, IT'S BECAUSE GOD IS PUNISHING ME.

GOD IS NOT IN A GOOD MOOD.

HA! HA! HA! HA! HA! HA! HA!

THE TRUTH

KEY VERSE

Psalm 145:8

"The Lord is merciful and compassionate, slow to get angry and filled with unfailing love."

God is love (1 John 4:8). 1 Corinthians 13:4-7 describes what love is like – so it is describing what God is like. Love (God) is patient and kind. He is patient with you. He is also quick to forgive when you make a mistake. The prodigal son made many mistakes, and his dad welcomed him home with a party and loving arms (Luke 15:11-32). God does that for us every day. His heart is to be kind to you.

The Bible talks over and over again about how God is slow to anger. He doesn't get mad with us every time we do something wrong. When we go through a hard time, God is there with us to help us. In fact, the Bible also says many times that God is quick to forgive – that's really good news! God is forgiving, and He washes our sins far, far away (Isaiah 55:7).

Remember that God is love, and God loves you. He not only loves you, He also really likes you! God delights in you. Delight means to take great joy in someone or something. Yes, God delights in you (Zephaniah 3:17).

WHAT CAN I SAY?

- God's not mad at me. He's madly in love with me.
- It is safe to run to God when I make a mistake.
- Jesus took God's anger for me on the cross.
- God delights in me!

WHAT CAN I DO?

- **Focus on God's kindness** - There are many stories of characters in the Bible that made mistakes. They could have thought God would be mad at them forever. As you think about this, see how many characters you can list that made mistakes, but God forgave them and used them powerfully.

- **Get creative with the truth** - Use the declarations above (or make up your own) to create a poem, rap, spoken word, or simple song about God being good, and recite it often. You can even make dance moves to go with it and teach it to your family. You could also make a piece of artwork that reminds you of God's patience, and hang it where you will see it often.

- **Picture it** - When you feel like God is mad, choose to come to Him. He is waiting with a smile on His face and welcoming arms. Use your imagination to picture a time when you messed up, and see God waiting to give you a big hug. Picture Him smiling at you. Remember that God loved you before you even knew Him, and He has never been mad at you.

GOD WON'T PROVIDE

You're out with your parents and you see this great new toy that you want. You look at your parents and ask them nicely, "Can I have that?" They look back at you and gently say, "We can't afford it." You are disappointed. You begin to wonder, are we okay? What else can't we afford? Will we have enough? Lies begin to swirl around in your head, and you start to think God won't provide for you. But wait, let's throw that lie to the ground, put on our Laughter Boots, and stomp it to bits!

LET'S STOMP THESE LIES TOO!

NO OTHER FAMILY HAS MONEY PROBLEMS.

GOD WILL NOT PROVIDE FOR MY FAMILY.

I CAN'T BE HAPPY UNTIL I HAVE EVERYTHING I WANT.

GOD GIVES BETTER GIFTS TO OTHER PEOPLE.

I SHOULD THROW A TEMPER TANTRUM
IF I CANNOT HAVE EVERYTHING I WANT.

THE TRUTH

KEY VERSE

Philippians
4:19

"And this
same God
who takes
care of me
will
supply all
your needs
from His
glorious
riches, which
have been
given to us in
Christ
Jesus."

God is always with us, He will never leave us, and He will provide all that we need. He even cares about the things we want (but we may not get them every time).

Have you ever watched birds gather their food? It isn't hard. They don't worry. Now picture a flower growing. It simply comes out of the ground, gets taller and taller, and one day all its leaves open into brilliant color, and people admire it. Jesus made that flower. He caused it to grow. He gave it everything it needed to make it so beautiful.

Jesus cares for you more than He cares for birds and flowers. He will watch over you in every way. You do not have to be afraid. This is good news (Matthew 6:30-33)!

Philippians 4:19 promises that God will supply all your needs according to "His glorious riches, which have been given to us in Christ Jesus." We are His children, and we get to receive His goodness, take care of what He gives us, and trust Him for the rest.

WHAT CAN I SAY?

- God is a good provider.
- My family will always have what we need.
- Things are getting better.

WHAT CAN I DO?

- **Remember how big God is -** In the Bible (and even today) there are so many stories about how God has provided for people in supernatural ways. One story is when the disciples were fishing in John 21. They hadn't caught anything all day. Then Jesus showed up, and they caught so many fish, they could not even lift them all into their boat (John 21:6). When we hear stories like this, we remember how big God is.

- **Get excited -** God wants to answer your prayers. Write your worries on paper and put them in a box. As you set the box on a table, imagine you are giving them to God. Ask Him what He wants to give you in return. Ask Him to show you His goodness and let Him speak to you about things you can get excited about!

- **Give something away -** Wow! This may sound crazy to you. Ask God to show you something you have that would bring joy to someone else. Give it to them, and know that you just made a difference. Our generosity to others causes blessings to increase in our own family (Luke 6:38).

TESTIMONIES

Emily loved to please people and was overly sensitive to what they thought of her. This meant that making decisions could be challenging for her. As an eleven-year-old girl, she even struggled to spend her allowance and often stated, "I just can't choose." Her mother suggested that she change her confession to "I am a great decision maker." A few weeks later, Emily and her mother went shopping for some last minute items for a trip they were going on. As they finished their shopping, Emily turned in amazement to her mother and said, "This declaring really works. I just made a whole lot of good decisions. I really am a great decision maker."

Ben was nine when he became convinced that he was bad at math and couldn't ever succeed in that class. His mother challenged him to change the way he believed by using the declaration, "God makes my math brain strong." Several weeks of declarations later, his math grades had improved and he was becoming confident in his math abilities. The complaining about math classes disappeared. By the following year, he was proud to be one of the top math students in his class.

Holly was seven when she noticed a girl in first grade spelling a word that she couldn't as a second grader. That was all it took for the lie that she was stupid to settle on her and steal her joy. Spelling practice became painful for her and her parents as she became increasingly convinced that she wasn't smart. Getting to the bottom of it wasn't easy, but finally it came out: "I don't think I'm smart." Mom and daughter wrote the offending lie on a tissue and flushed it down the toilet together. Next they wrote a simple declaration of "Holly is smart" on a piece of sparkly paper that was put at the end of Holly's bed. By the next day at spelling practice, Holly was back to singing and dancing as she spelled out her words. She now works at a grade level above her own in spelling.

Grace is a pretty eight-year-old girl. In her classroom at school, they were talking about how the enemy lies to them. As the teacher led them in a time of recognizing lies they were believing about themselves, Grace realized that she believed she was ugly. The teacher had the kids pretend to stomp the lies and they asked God to tell them the truth. Grace heard the Lord tell her how beautiful she was. With a beaming smile, she told the teacher at the end of class, "Now I know I am beautiful again."

MY DAILY DECLARATIONS

Declarations help us build our faith! When we believe them, we will be ready to receive even more of God's goodness!

1. My prayers are powerful!
2. God loves to provide for me.
3. I am free from sin and alive in Him.
4. My health gets better every day.
5. God has supernatural protection for me.
6. I am great at relationships.
7. Because God is with me, the people around me experience His love and power.
8. Because of Jesus, I am loved 100% and super blessed.
9. My family is blessed.
10. I recognize and laugh at the devil's lies.

Hearing truth helps us grow in faith. We must have faith to believe God's promises when negative things feel and sound true. We say declarations out loud to grow our faith.

1. My words direct my life.
2. God is on my side. I can't be beaten!
3. I am a leader, I have great ideas, and God makes me powerful.
4. When I speak truth, my faith grows, and I become who God made me to be.
5. I think right thoughts, I speak words of life, and I make good decisions even when it is tough.
6. God will use me today to release His power and love to the people around me.
7. Today will be the best day yet!

To move mountains with Jesus, we need to speak to things. Let's say these!

1. Because I love Jesus, angels are working for me.
2. Bad things are turned away from me because of Jesus' protection.
3. I am a person of peace and bring peace to those around me.
4. I tell tiredness, sadness, and fear to leave in Jesus' name.
5. This day is a blessed day. I can't wait to see how God's goodness shows up!

POWERFUL PHRASES FOR PARENTS

"WHO TOLD YOU THAT?"

Many times, our past is speaking to us things that are not true. When we hear phrases that cause hopelessness about our future, we have to ask ourselves, "Who told you that?" If Jesus told you, through the Bible or by speaking it directly to you, you can trust it is the truth. If you learned to believe it another way and it isn't what God says, then it's a lie. If what you believe isn't what you would encourage your friend with, and if it doesn't bring hope, then it is a lie.

"WHAT DOES GOD'S WORD SAY?"

Just because something feels true does not make it the truth. Sometimes kids feel like friends don't like them because they didn't smile at them. It feels like they stopped being friends, but the truth is that they are just having a bad day because their dog died or someone yelled at them. Lies can often feel really true, especially when we have believed them for a long time. When we become great lie detectives, we know that feelings don't make something true. The Word of God is the truth that we can live our lives by.

"THE JOY OF THE LORD IS MY STRENGTH!"

No one can steal our joy. It comes from God, and He gives it freely to us. Joy is God's way of giving us strength. There are always going to be hard days. The good news is that we get to choose how we respond to them. When we choose joy, strength is released to us to deal with the hard times. We get to choose to be joyful.

"THERE IS ALWAYS A SOLUTION."

Sometimes, especially as a child, it seems like there is no way out of a hard situation. No matter what we try to do, nothing seems to change. The truth is that there is always a way through it. Luke 1:37 says that nothing is impossible with God. When we choose to believe that there is a solution, we are prepared to find that solution with God.

"CELEBRATE PROGRESS, NOT PERFECTION."

There is always something to celebrate. While we are still on a journey, celebrating our growth is a key tool in defeating the enemy's lies. Look intentionally for areas where you have already grown. The goal in fighting lies is not to be perfect, but to keep growing.

IGNITING HOPE RESOURCES

LET'S JUST LAUGH AT THAT
BY STEVE BACKLUND

Our hope level is an indicator of whether we are believing truth or lies. Truth creates hope and freedom, but believing lies brings hopelessness and restriction. We can have great theology but still be powerless because of deception about the key issues of life. Many of these self-defeating mindsets exist in our subconscious and have never been identified. This book exposes numerous falsehoods and reveals truth that makes us free. Get ready for a joy-infused adventure into hope-filled living.

DECLARATIONS
BY STEVE BACKLUND

"Nothing happens in the kingdom unless a declaration is made." Believers everywhere are realizing the power of declarations to empower their lives. *Declarations* shares 30 biblical reasons for declaring truth over every area of life. Steve Backlund and his team also answer common objections and concerns to the teaching about declarations. The revelation this book carries will help you to set the direction your life will go. Get ready for 30 days of powerful devotions and declarations that will convince you that life is truly in the power of the tongue.

Find more resources including books, group studies, and declarations lists at *ignitinghope.com*

ADDITIONAL RESOURCES

KINGDOM TOOLS FOR TEACHING
BY JANINE MASON

The Creator of the universe has His eye on the education systems of the world and, in particular, on your classroom. He longs to have His presence expressed in every school across the globe, influencing faculty and students alike. His presence in schools is not illegal though mentioning His name may be. *Kingdom Tools for Teaching; Heavenly Strategies for Real Classrooms* brings inspiration and practical tools to empower and activate teachers in bringing the Kingdom of God to their classrooms.
Are you ready to change the way you teach?

I DECLARE POSTER

Commonly known as Bethel Church's "Offering Reading #4", this powerful declaration originated in Bethel Church's Children's Ministry! This poster features powerful truths such as "God is in a good mood," "I am important," "Jesus' blood paid for everything," and "Nothing is impossible." At 18"x 24", this poster is the perfect size to be hung in a child's bedroom or a children's ministry department. Great for ALL ages, as these truths transcend all ages – children and adults!

For more excellent resources, including curriculum for children's ministry, visit *sethdahl.com*

Made in the USA
Charleston, SC
05 August 2015